Mexican Gardens & Patios

Sandy Baum

Schiffer Publishing Ltd®

4880 Lower Valley Road, Atglen, PA 19310

Schiffer Books are available at special discounts for bulk purchases for sales promotions or premiums. Special editions, including personalized covers, corporate imprints, and excerpts can be created in large quantities for special needs. For more information contact the publisher:

Published by Schiffer Publishing Ltd.
4880 Lower Valley Road
Atglen, PA 19310
Phone: (610) 593-1777; Fax: (610) 593-2002
E-mail: Info@schifferbooks.com

For the largest selection of fine reference books on this and related subjects, please visit our web site at **www.schifferbooks.com**
We are always looking for people to write books on new and related subjects. If you have an idea for a book please contact us at the above address.

This book may be purchased from the publisher.
Include $5.00 for shipping.
Please try your bookstore first.
You may write for a free catalog.

In Europe, Schiffer books are distributed by
Bushwood Books
6 Marksbury Ave.
Kew Gardens
Surrey TW9 4JF England
Phone: 44 (0) 20 8392 8585; Fax: 44 (0) 20 8392 9876
E-mail: info@bushwoodbooks.co.uk
Website: www.bushwoodbooks.co.uk

Contents

Acknowledgments		4
Introduction		5
1.	Courtyards	6
2.	Outdoor Living Spaces	13
3.	Patio Gates, Doors & Windows	27
4.	Outdoor Dining	38
5.	Rooftop Terraces	48
6.	Patio Bars	60
7.	Rooftop Shelters	64
8.	Garden Walks & Stairways	71
9.	Patterns & Paving	86
10.	Courtyard Fountains	93
11.	Garden Sculpture	106
12.	Outdoor Garden Lighting	122
13.	Swimming Pools	126
14.	Outdoor Fireplaces	130
15.	Aquatic Gardens	135
16.	Garden Color	141
17.	Outdoor Accessories	152
Glossary		155
Resources		156
Bibliography		160

Acknowledgments

San Miguel has been my home now for over four years and in those four years, I've made many friends who have been very supportive of my endeavor to bring to the public photography books on San Miguel. Working on this book, as with others about San Miguel, has been a joy and a pleasurable experience, mostly because of the new friends and acquaintances I was fortunate to meet along the way.

I hope you, the reader, enjoy this journey behind these closed doors and walls that line the streets of San Miguel, a journey to which the typical visitor to San Miguel will not be invited. This book would not have been possible without the editorial input of friends and neighbors: Betsy January, probably my most vocal editor and critic; Alegria Skully who, with her husband, Mike Skully, have spent hours pouring over my text; Phil Jeffrey, an English major when she was in college, keeps correcting both my English as well as my poor Spanish; Leona Camp who worked on some of my earlier text, and Nancy Newton, when she is in town between her world travels. Susan Page was one of my early moral supporters with her comment, "Do you know how lucky you are?" Lulu Torbert was also a supporter who volunteered to go over my early material. A special thanks goes to my two editors at Schiffer Publishing, Ltd, Nancy Schiffer and Tina Skinner, whose patience and foresight helped bring forth this book. And finally, a great big thanks to all those homeowners who were kind enough to open their doors each Sunday for the House & Garden tour sponsored by the Biblioteca Publica, a weekly fund raising event for the many programs that exist at the library, programs aimed at educating the Mexican children of San Miguel. I thank you all.

Be inspired to create your own Mexican style garden and patio after you step into a little-known world of magic, mystery, and color, behind the walls of some of the most exclusive living areas in town, to a world where the typical visitor is not an invited guest. This world was created by each of the homeowners with a bent for the exotic. No two gardens are the same, and their variety reflects the creative effort brought to bear on these delightful spaces, always with the added ingenuity of the Mexican workers.

In many towns throughout Mexico, houses still retain blank exteriors facing the street, some with an occasional window. However, once beyond these canyon-forming walls, one is exposed to interior gardens and patios alive with rainbows of color. Here the front of the house may be one story, but once inside the entrance, a visitor might be exposed to two or more stories of living space, probably with gardens, patios, a rooftop terrace, and a fantastic view of the downtown skyline.

Chapter 1.
Courtyards

The courtyard covers the entire front of the lot, with the covered entry along the side of the courtyard providing a shaded outdoor area.

This courtyard is surrounded
on three sides with doors and
windows, allowing daylight into
the far recesses of the residence.
Since most homes are on a "zero"
lot line, all the interior daylight
comes from open courtyards.

The furniture at this entry has
a formal arrangement. The paving is a combination of *saltillo*
paver and stones set into a bed
of concrete.

The home surrounds a courtyard in an "L" shape, with a two-car garage occupying the far left side. Another patio for entertaining is located beyond the long (right) side of the "L."

The courtyard viewed from the upper patio. Individual, smooth rock paving was laid by hand.

Cantera stone paving surrounds this classic *cantera* fountain.

This second-floor courtyard has a classic, clean, contemporary look.

Grass between the pavers softens
the look and permits a cooler
daytime temperature.

Wrought iron furniture
provides a place to relax
in this typical outdoor
Mexican setting.

Most courtyards have pavers, a
variety of plants, and fountains
to provide a quiet ambience.

The size of the fountain is not as critical as is the sound it makes, masking the extraneous noises.

This fountain in the heart of a restaurant courtyard provides a soothing atmosphere for diners.

Chapter 2.

Outdoor
Living Spaces

A long outdoor living space
leads from the street entry
directly into the kitchen
beyond.

The round table top and chairs are on matching *equipal* bases.

No matter the make or shape of the furniture, cushions are most welcome for a more comfortable experience.

Cushions are a welcome addition to this rustic seating.

This outdoor haven is away from the street noises while basking in the sun.

The black and white striped chaise lounge cushions are a nice contrast to the red walls.

The wrought iron railing does a radius turn around the gnarled mesquite tree, providing an interesting relationship with the patio space.

This outdoor fireplace provides some warmth during the evening winter chills.

This outdoor living space provides a respite from the dark interiors.

The *equipal* chairs surround a hand-carved table while the barbeque in the background awaits lighting for expected company invited to dinner.

These *equipal* chairs have white cushions that make dining at this table quite comfortable.

This outdoor living space leads to the casita around the corner to the left, adjacent to the main house on the right. The door in the corner leads to the kitchen. The *saltillo* paving is a universal pattern used in Mexico.

No two outdoor living spaces are ever the same. This outdoor area leads from the kitchen to outside dining.

This seating area provides an outdoor respite after pruning the garden.

The outdoor dining area is on a raised platform in the distance.

Tastes in materials and style dictate a personal environment. You can tell a lot about a person by the environment they create for themselves.

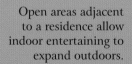

Open areas adjacent to a residence allow indoor entertaining to expand outdoors.

This open courtyard
provides additional
space for expanding
indoor entertaining
and a quiet evening of
dining.

Another hideaway
providing a quiet
atmosphere away from
street noises.

Outdoor space is sometimes at a premium. Shade is wherever you can find a place to put your furniture.

This outdoor space with a deep overhang provides a great entertaining area come rain or shine.

Color is important in this large open space for providing a quiet ambience.

The old hand-hewn mesquite chairs are a throwback to chairs from the Appalachia Mountains, and are much more comfortable with cushions.

A relaxing patio area is shaded by several older trees. The clay sculptured rabbit on the low table was made by the owner.

Open areas adjacent to
a residence allow indoor
entertaining to flow
outdoors.

Soft colors play a large part in the quiet ambience one finds on any patio.

Not all adjacent spaces are for entertaining. This quiet seating area is just outside the owner's bedroom.

Chapter 3

Patio Gates, Doors & Windows

Wrought iron design has no limits when it comes to gates that protect access to one's property, from the simplest to curlicues with circles.

This door leads to a narrow balcony giving support to a wrought iron railing and potted plants attached to it.

A see-through wrought iron gate to keep the animals inside.

A creatively designed gate.

This gate is for visual effect, since the house occupies both sides.

A gate within an enclosed arch above leads to a private residence.

This transom resembles half of an Old West wagon wheel.

Wrought iron plays a major part in decorating windows, both as a security feature as well as a balcony railing, while enclosing access to property as a gate.

This short, wrought iron railing is outside a second floor bedroom.

Decorative gates maintain security while enabling passersby a look in.

The rectangular patio door is set into a rounded archway, with side lights providing additional daylight into the bedroom.

Window design is always a concern when it comes to feeling secure.

Another example of window security.

This glass and wrought iron door hides a storage area under the stairs.

Three separate exterior wooden doors serve the same design purpose.

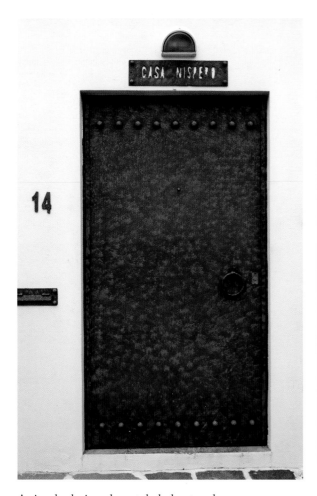

A simply designed, metal-clad entry door.

French doors provide an abundant amount of light to brighten the adjacent room next to this patio.

This double-leaf wooden door leads to the *casita* in the lower level.

An old fashioned brass door knocker on an entry door.

A protective fence on a two-way small window.

No two exterior openings ever seem the same. This opening required a double-leaf French door with an arched transom above.

Contemporary hardware on a glass patio door.

More pots (*macetas*) hang from this wrought iron balcony railing.

Window pots (*macetas*) come in a variety of sizes and finishes; the choice is up to the homeowner.

Far left:
This narrow door gives access to a utility closet under the stairs.

Left:
This narrow door leads to a colorful, yellow-tiled bathroom under the second floor terrace.

Chapter 4.
Outdoor Dining

The color blue is certainly prominent in this traditional patio.

A table is set for a full-course meal. Notice the placemats that may indicate fish on the menu.

Soft-cushioned chairs make dining outside a comfortable experience surrounded by a profusion of orange bougainvilleas.

This dining area is surrounded by a deep growth of colorful plants enhanced by a variety of potted green plants.

The raised deck affords diners a view to distant rolling hills beyond the lower adjacent wall.

This roof deck provides a lovely view while guests enjoy a relaxing time in the sun.

A round table with green umbrella seems to be the preferred outdoor dining furniture.

Shade is sometimes at a premium, but anywhere outside is great for dining.

These metal chairs are more comfortable with light blue cushions that add a cooling look.

Round tables seem to fit
everywhere comfortably.

Metal chairs are far more
comfortable with seat
cushions. Here the garden
surrounds the eating area.

The brightly painted furniture offers sharp contrast to green foliage and a yellow fish in this garden.

The blue metal table and chairs with all-weather white cushions can remain outdoors during the rainy season.

The seating area is under a roof for any kind of weather.

Typical bare-bones *equipal* chairs with leather seats and surrounding backs have been painted red.

Classic wooden folding chairs without cushions are comfortable for most people. The enormous umbrella looks protective.

Equipal chairs come in a variety of finish materials, while their basic design has not changed since they were first made. These have both a padded seat and surrounding back.

Another group of *equipal* chairs of different materials.

The blue tablecloth is striking against grey walls in this attractive interior space.

Chapter 5.
Rooftop Terraces

The unique staircase has an unusual railing. This is not for the faint of heart, but does not waste space on a small patio.

This rooftop patio enjoys the sun all day because there are no buildings to block the rays. The sound of water in the fountain blocks the street noise.

Since this rooftop terrace is covered, the seating takes on the feelings of a living room, with soft cushions and no concern for rain.

Outdoor seating that is carefully planned has less concern for the weather.

A fine view of San Miguel can be had from most of the town's rooftop terraces.

The sweeping rooftop patio is shaded by an enormous umbrella, to ward off intense sunshine at the 6000-foot elevation.

A profusion of potted plants on this patio brings the rooftop garden into view from the bedroom.

A row of potted plants thrive on the rooftop, with a white umbrella for shade.

This rooftop terrace has multiple-sized pots containing a profusion of green plants.

These *equipal* style chairs have tufted, soft cushions over the leather seat.

A colorful wooden folding chair adds comfortable seating, with or without cushions.

This cozy brick corner is shielded from two sides with a partial roof.

Just for soaking up some sun.

Under roof, this outdoor furniture can remain inside the enclosure.

A silent cleric is the focal
point at the patio with
desert plants.

An *equipal* chair and bench occupy this conversation area and offers comfortable seating in front of the outdoor fireplace.

A rounded seating area follows the curve of the wall behind.

A mix of furniture styles and table surfaces add variety to this narrow patio.

This rooftop terrace had a magnificent view of the downtown skyline before surrounding trees matured.

ROOFTOP TERRACES

With changing seasons and an abundance of rain during summer months, metal chairs provide ideal seating on these four rooftop terraces.

The view from this patio is outstanding. Metal tables and chairs remain here throughout the year.

Terraces, courtyards, and patios have a plethora of pots (*macetas*) for many native plant materials.

Chapter 6.
Patio Bars

An outdoor barbeque is a convenient meeting place for dinner guests.

This bar is in partial shade, to help keep ice cubes from melting.

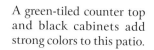

Besides the built-in barbecue, it's nice to have a bar on balmy nights that invite outdoor dining.

A green-tiled counter top and black cabinets add strong colors to this patio.

Behind the barbecue are a *talavera*-tiled counter top, back splash, and *talavera* platter embedded in the wall.

You can always find a creative use for space under the stairs.

Chapter 7.

Rooftop Shelters

This structure was a design statement by the architect.

This typical rooftop shelter was constructed with *cantera* columns, wooden beams and rafters, and a *saltillo* tile roof.

A simply designed, open roof offers less shade from the sun and covering from the rain, but is a pleasant outdoor retreat.

The hand-carved columns supporting this roof shelter came from the State of Michoacan.

Another typical lean-to roof structure has a supporting wall and two columns to hold the main beam.

Here, three wooden columns support the roof structure, with the fourth corner being held-up by a diagonal wall.

A free-standing roof structure has four brick column supports.

This typical roof has a long beam supporting the rafter extensions.

Similar to a floating hyperbolic paraboloid, this free-form roof structure was boldly designed.

This free-standing roof structure is supported by four *cantera* columns.

Chapter 8.

Garden Walks & Stairways

Some stairs require hand railings while others do not. In Mexico, the use of a handrail is left up to the owner, since many jurisdictions lack building codes that dictate safety requirements.

This walkway, with just a few steps, did not require handrails.

These shallow steps lead to a patio between two building extensions.

A cast-in-place concrete and stone stairway to the second level fits snugly into the corner.

In Mexico, many stairways have handrails on the outside or inside of the steps, but never on both.

Multi-colored walls surround this outdoor stairway that leads to a second floor terrace.

This wide stairway, with a hand rail down the center, is lined with a variety of potted plants.

Talavera tile was laid into the concrete stairway risers. Potted plants hang from the handrail.

A different railing design was used on this stairway to the second level.

Here, plants in *talavera* pots mirror the *talavera* tiled stairway risers, and climbing vines reach up a wall.

In a confined space, this stairway maintains a continuous ninety-degree angle along its downward flow.

Lined by a plethora of potted plants, a stairway leads to the entry door.

A sweeping stairway leads from the street to the first floor entry, providing a magnificent view from its sloping lot.

The *talavera*-tiled Moroccan arch welcomes visitors to a wonderland of make-believe.

Cascading vines cover a wall as potted plants bloom in various colors along the top.

The stairway in this courtyard leads to a second floor office.

Pre-cut *cantera* treads join fill-in stone risers.

The *cantera* treads and risers on these stairs will last a lifetime.

These four photos show a uniquely designed iron handrail that is both functional and pleasing to the eye. It proves that not all handrails need to be solid brick and concrete.

Cantera treads with *talavera* tile-faced risers are the design theme for this stairway.

Handrails are designed to flow with the stairways, as seen at this curving *talavera*-faced stairway with a blue handrail.

A garden walk with plenty of plants.

This meandering brick stairway follows the hillside contour.

This two-story stairway hugs the building on the way to the second floor.

A combination of blue handrail and blue and white *talavera*-tiled risers makes a good contrast with the *saltillo* treads.

You can never tell what you may find during your walks on *cantera* pavers through this park-like setting.

Garden walks and stairways have a variety of design shapes, materials, and colors. Be very careful when you walk on cobblestones.

This limited space required a creative design using colorful materials and pots (*macetas*) with plants.

Chapter 9.
Patterns
& Paving

Stacked bricks form a screen
behind which landscape
materials and tools are
hidden.

This honeycombed ceiling creates diffused daylight for the room below.

A pleasing, geometric paving pattern is seen from the second floor balcony of this residence. The courtyard space dictated this radial pattern instead of the traditional rectangular design.

The lower wooden post-and-beam construction is not the typical roof design in Mexico today.

Non-structural wooden beams are used as a design element, partially hiding the round skylight. This design is sometimes used as a lattice to shade the sun's rays.

This wooden post-and-beam layout enhances an otherwise typical concrete-and-brick construction. Creative design has melded various materials into a pleasing finish.

Round peeler logs were used here with a herringbone pattern of lay-in wooden slates, again combining materials.

A circular set of skylights in this bedroom ceiling creates a striking pattern of light rays as the sun passes over.

Right:
A creative wall hanging, with a variety of design shapes, forms interesting patterns.

Far right:
This is a typical paving pattern using *saltillo* tiles with pebbles in between. This system is not only pleasing to the eye, but aids in the drainage of water.

A combination of *talavera* tiles in a field of solid tiles is quite colorful.

This handsome ceiling is on the interior of a residence. Oval exterior walls supporting the roof structure contain clerestory windows, which give this ceiling so much bright daylight.

A detail of the colorful *talavera* pattern in the solid tan background.

Patterns are endless and most designers have a creative shape always at their fingertips. The field in this design uses *cantera* wedges, while stone chips were used as in-fill.

Another *talavera* tile is used with a second pattern to form a border surrounded by *saltillo* tiles.

Cut granite blocks form interesting patterns in these two floors.

Chapter 10.

Courtyard Fountains

Just the sound of moving, cool,
refreshing water can be hypnotic
and provide an escape from
surrounding sounds we find
distracting in our daily lives.

This angel statue pours water into a blue-tiled fountain.

An octagonal *cantera* courtyard fountain sits on a multi-colored *cantera* platform surrounded by a radiating pattern of cobblestones. The interior of the fountain has *talavera* tile in two different patterns.

Another octagonal fountain is made of concrete and lined with tile. The stem from which the water cascades is unusual.

This round *cantera* fountain is lined with *talavera* tile and surrounded by a *cantera* step. Active fountains produce pleasant sounds that block out extraneous noises.

This faux fountain is three niches backed by mirrors and with sculptures, alluding to a view on the other side of the wall.

Just the steady drip of water can have a mesmerizing effect. This fountain is in the center of an outside courtyard.

Above:
An interior fountain provides ambient sound throughout the home as well as needed moisture during dry, warm days.

Top right:
A circular outdoor fountain acts as a needed watering hole for birds.

Bottom right:
This multi-colored *talavera* tile-encased fountain reflects colorful house colors.

A security window is part of this fountain design.

Most of these fountains are sound generators filtering out extraneous street or neighbor noises.

This creative fountain is of special interest.

The fountain is made from *cantera*.

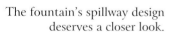

The fountain's spillway design
deserves a closer look.

This *cantera* fountain creates a stepping-stone effect of cascading water.

A round *cantera* fountain rests in a field of cobblestones.

These marble-faced columns have flat stones set between them. Falling water creates a different sound as it cascades downward.

A simple fountain has water cascading from a projecting shelf surrounded by *cantera*.

Fountain design possibilities are endless. This fountain's spray is adjustable.

The next three photographs show a courtyard with a classical *cantera* fountain that has blue *talavera* tile facing the interior of the bowl.

A more contemporary wall fountain has water cascading from several shelves into a shallow pool lined with tile.

This massive fountain is tucked into a small area with a *cantera* fish sculpture providing the water source.

This more classical fountain has two *cantera* fish providing the falling water.

This modern fountain will be plumbed to provide flowing water.

Chapter 11.
Garden Sculpture

This portrait of a musician
was carved from *cantera*.

This burro was made from wood scraps and driftwood.

A sun carving decorates the door of this private residence.

This bronze penguin sculpture was donated by a local artist and is resting in the Parque Juarez.

A Mexican family of three resides in the garden.

An artist's rendition of a
fine feathered friend.

This colorful chicken figure
is at rest in the garden.

A carved *cantera* fish rests
on a garden pedestal.

A school of three
swimming bronze
fish.

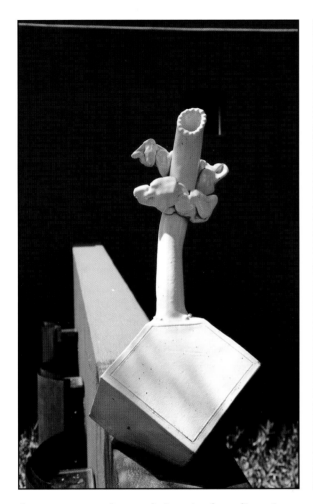

A contemporary abstract design stimulates discussion.

Both of these open-minded ladies (head vases) are the creations of a local sculptress who works in clay, bronze, and multi-media.

The amusing king of the jungle was carved from *cantera*.

This bronze cat sculpture sits in a quiet corner of the patio.

A sculpture represents a former Spanish soldier who seems to have drunk too much wine from his bota.

This carved *cantera* fish oversees the swimming pool.

This bronze turtle does not move fast within the children's playground at Juarez Parque.

A wooden carving of a skinny man with a hat.

One of the mythical creatures carved from *cantera*.

A multiple candle holder for those dark nights without electricity.

A wary Spanish soldier still carrying his tools of war.

Several *cantera* sculptures perched around a *talavera* balcony in the garden.

A *talavera* pig seems airborne, suspended from a wire hanger.

This carved owl sculpture
stands over two feet tall.

Kinetic sculptures add delightful
movement to the gardens.

Movement is also conveyed
by this stone sculpture.

A colorful, bottle-shaped
whimsy for fun.

A large and dramatic *talavera* fish is actually a ceramic heater.

In the midst of the garden we find a slumbering *hombre*.

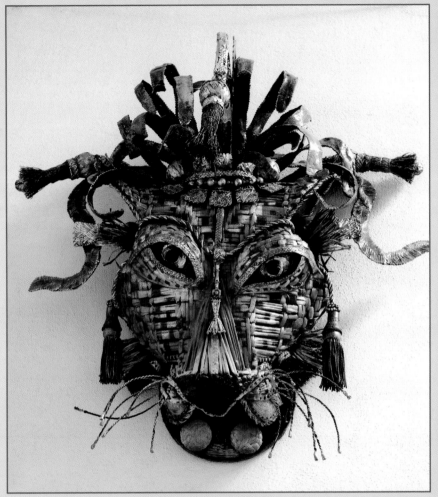

The woven straw mask of a cat from the jungle adds drama to any space.

A solid wooden wheel with a square hole for a shaft now makes an interesting ornament in this garden.

Chapter 12

Outdoor Garden Lighting

Most of the garden lighting included on the following pages are modern, self-contained units with solar batteries that require no wiring. The batteries store energy when the sun shines and can either be switched on when desired or left on to shine silently when darkness commands.

This light does require wiring to function.

An oriental style lantern fitted with an electric light.

A differently designed shape that is powered by the sun.

Another oriental style light fixture with solar collectors on the top.

An electric wired lantern to light the gardens.

An electric fixture for soft, ambient light.

Even a candle-powered outdoor light.

The top of a typical fixture showing the solar collectors.

This is a low-voltage light fixture.

A differently designed solar light for the gardens.

Another brass fixture with the solar collectors exposed.

Chapter 13.
Swimming Pools

Swimming pool styles depend on the whims of the owners and characteristics of the site. Here a pool is an integral part of the garden.

This lap pool is surrounded by palm trees planted far enough from the pool as not to drop their seeds or fronds into the water.

More for soaking than swimming, this is a Jacuzzi-type pool.

With recirculating water, this pool has a beautiful view overlooking San Miguel.

This lap pool has recirculating water creating a waterfall at the side.

Chapter 14.
Outdoor Fireplaces

More a decorative sculpture than a unit for a patio, this attractive fireplace is located just outside the entry door to a residence in the countryside.

This magnificent fireplace will give a little heat and light as soon as the gas line is attached from the propane tank.

A Mexican ceramic bottle-shaped space heater for an individual room is used here as patio decoration.

This good looking corner fireplace appears to be a wood-burning facility, but on closer inspection even the logs sitting on the hearth are recognized as non-burning.

This is a typical Mexican
designed fireplace lined
with bricks.

This real brick fireplace has a chimney to carry wood-burning smoke to the outside.

This is a classic design,
probably without a flue.

Chapter 15

Aquatic Gardens

Some of the aquatic gardens shown here have plants growing within, while others have plants surrounding or nearby the water. Small water environments have a soothing effect on everyone.

The water lilies and papyrus are softly combined in this aquatic garden.

Potted plants sitting in water make plant exchange and cleaning easy.

This kidney shaped body of water has stepping stones at the end of the walking path.

A Volga boatman sits in dry dock waiting for the water to rise.

Here, a round pool has a variety of plants along with some goldfish.

A corner water feature is surrounded with various plants.

Some aquatic gardens are like quiet sentries showing no movement, while others provide bubbling water that creates a sound filter.

This meandering pool falls in elevation and has two bubblers and a variety of plants.

This example has a
small water source but
a big voice that acts
as a sound filter.

Here a self-contained,
quiet garden pool
shows no movement
but is the focal point of
the terrace.

Chapter 16.

Garden Color

The flower shapes and their colors are pervasive in Mexico's high altitudes that seem to bring out the best features in any garden. Many semi-tropical plant varieties grow well here.

Clusters of red lantanas
are common in Mexico.

A field of yellow cascades
along this hillside.

Geraniums grow easily in Mexican sunshine.

The bird of paradise, Strelitzia, adds a dramatic feature throughout the country.

Members of the Tipuana flower family are pretty and fragrant.

Flame vine grows profusely in the mountain regions.

Hydrangea is a favorite common plant with blossoms of pastel blue, pink, purple or white.

African Daisy adds a nice accent in many gardens.

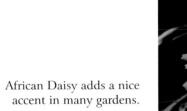

African Daisy has the look and glow of the sun.

Vinca in many colors
grows well in Mexico.

This field of orange Vincas includes a lavender volunteer.

A member of the lily family makes a nice border material.

White Vinca is pristine
and easy to grow.

A pretty field of orange
Vincas tumbles down a
Mexican hillside.

This colorful backyard goes on and on.

Bougainvilleas climb the side of this house.

Red peppers on the vine are ready to heat up a good Mexican dish.

A lone butterfly stopped for awhile to savor the fragrances.

Yellow daisies look like the hot Mexican sun.

A rose in her hair is a favorite accent to any lady's costume.

Bougainvilleas rest on this garden wall.

Bougainvillea colors are intense at a 6000-foot elevation.

Chapter 17.
Outdoor Accesories

A sun of woven fabric is colorful and interesting with its intricate design and pattern.

Not all birdcages were meant to be homes for real feathered friends.

Candleholders can bring a warm glow to any patio.

An outdoor fire pit can have a good psychological effect besides keeping you warm.

A multi-light candleholder can bring drama to any patio or garden.

A nicely planted garden patio can be a fun place to relax in the sun.

Even little birds need to be fed and their feeders can be delightful features to a patio.

This simple bench/sculpture invites you to rest in this patio garden.

Glossary

Agua. Water
Ala derecha. To the right
Alberca. Pool
Amigo. Friend
Arboles. Trees
Arcada. Arcade
Armario. Cabinet
Arquitecto. Architect
Artes. Arts
Azul. Blue
Azulejo. Tile

Balaustrada. Balustrade
Banco. Bench
Bandidos. Bandits
Baño. Bathroom
Boveda. Vault
Brasero. Brazier

Canalon. Gutter
Cantera. Volcanic stone
Cantina. Bar
Cartas. Letters
Casa. House
Cascada. Waterfall
Casita. Small house
Chimenea. Fireplace
Clavo. Nail
Cobalto. Colbalt
Cochera. Garage
Cocina. Kitchen

Comedor. Dining room
Comoda. Chest of drawers
Cornisa. Cornice
Corredor. Corridor
Cristo. Christ
Cupula. Cupola or dome

Entrada. Entryway
Equipal. Pigskin furniture
Escalera. Stair or ladder

Fabrica. Fabricate
Fachada. Facade
Flores. Flowers
Fuenta. Fountain

Hierro. Iron
Hombre. Man

Iglesia. Church
Iluminacion. Lighting

Jardin. Garden
Jarrones. Large jars

Laja. Flat rock
Llamador. Door

Nicho. Niche

Ojo. Eye

Petateyes. Reed mats
Petatillo. A thin brick
Pilar. Pillar
Portal. Foyer
Portico. Covered porch at entry
Porton. Large door
Postigo. Small door usually inside another door
Puerta. Door

Que Pasa. Whats happening

Recamara. Bedroom
Reja. Iron grating or railing
Retablo. Religious painting

Sala. Living room
Santo. Saint
Silla. Chair
Sillon. Couch

Tablero. Panel of tiles
Talavera. Hand-painted, twice fired, tin-glazed earthen ware
Troje. Wooden house

Vestibulo. Hall or public lobby
Viga. Beam or girder

Zaguan. Passage from street to inner courtyard
Zocalo. Baseboard

Resources

The following services are within San Miguel proper or ouside the town's perimeter but within the greater metropolitan area.

Food & Tabletop

Bonanza
Mesones 43
152 1260
A complete in-town supermarket, with hard-to-find imported ítems.

De Talavera
Puebla No. 60 esq.
Tamaulipas
Delores Hidalgo, Gto.
(418) 182 0749
An extensive line of *talavera* dinnerware.

La Buena Vida
Hernandez Macias 72
152 2211
Bakery & Cafe
Natural whole grain breads, French baguettes, and unique pastries.

La Europea
Canal 13
152 2003
An extensive selection of wines and spirits.

Maxi Vinos
Zacateros 86
152 2219
A good selection of wines and spirits.

Petitfour
Mesones 99
154 4010
Pastry shop, bar, and café.
Homemade chocolates, cakes, pies, and French pastries.

Furniture

Arden Casa de Muebles
Libr. Celaya a Delores 26
154 8010
Furniture and home-decor accessories.

Camila
Sollano 30
152 2697
Antique furniture, etched glass, custom made linens & table cloths.

Casa Canal
Canal 3
152 0479
Hand carved furniture.

Casa del Inquisidor
Aldama 1
154 6868
Household accessories and an extensive hardware selection.

Casa Marie Luisa
Ancha Sn Antonio 26
152 2983
Furniture and home-decor accessories.

Coba Art Décor
Juarez 7
154 7516
Interior design, accessories, and fine furniture from India.

Colección Cuatro Vientos
Sollano 31
154 9132
Furniture and home-decor accessories.

C. Dewayne Youts
Fabrica la Aurora
152 5481
Manufacturing of wood and iron furniture, 17th century reproductions, custom kitchens, and accessories.

El Progresso
Road to Delores Hidalgo
(418) 120 3048
Hand-crafted furniture.

Evos
Hernandez Macias 55
152 0813
Classic San Miguel-style home furnishings, Spanish Colonial furniture, imported sofas, upholstered furniture, fabrics, and oriental rugs.

Finca
Fabrica la Aurora
154 8323
Furniture, accessories, and interiors.

Hacienda la Diligencia
Hernandez Macias 118
152 1626
Custom furniture made to your design and specifications.

Manuel Padron
Santa Clara
progresso2004@prodigy.com.mx
Hand-crafted furniture.

Marcia Bland Brown
Hacienda Calderón
044 415 153 3176
Furniture design & manufacturing, antiques, interior & architectural design, and restoration.

Namuh Collection
Camino Alcocer Km 2.2
154 8080
Indoor/outdoor furniture and
accessories from Asia.

Shops

Antigua Casa Canela
Umaran 20
152 1880
Antiques, Colonial art, and
home-décor accessories.

Artes de México
Calzada de la Aurora 47
152 0764
Mexican arts and crafts, tin
ornaments, Colonial furniture,
and folk art.

ArtesMéxico
Zapateros 81A
154 8531
Quality hand-wrought copper.

Azulejos Talavera Cortes S.A.de C.V.
Aldama 18
Delores Hidalgo, C.I.N., GTO.,
México
(418) 182 1168
Finest glazed *talavera* tiles for
floor finishing as well as an infinite
range of accessories.

Buenas Noches
Fabrica la Aurora
154 9624
Fine bed and
bath furnishings.

Cantadora
Fabrica la Aurora
154 8302
Cantera, fireplaces, columns, door
frames, and decorative accessories.

Carrillo Vertix Hermanos
Puebla No. 54
Delores Hidalgo, C.I.N., GTO.,
México
(418) 182 0122
Talavera tiles, traditional and
Barcelona murals, and accessories.

Casa Coloniales
Canal 36
152 0286
Furniture, upholstery, fabrics, trim,
pillows, spreads, curtains,
rugs, chandeliers, sconces, stone
ornaments, and gifts.

Casa Roberto
Libr a Queretaro 35
152 8620
Lighting, ceiling fans, water filters,
purifiers, radiant heaters, and
fireplace accessories.

Galería Tesoro
Recreo 8B
154 5595
Folk art and home-decor
accessories.

Icpalli
Correo 43
152 1236
Fabric for interior design,
window treatment, furniture,
and home accessories.

Icons
Pila Seca 3
152 5762
Traditional Byzantine
images.

Ilunina San Miguel
Calzada de la Luz 51
154 7643
Commercial &
residential lighting,
chandeliers, lamps,
and sconces.

Lan Art
Ancha de San Antonio
152 1566
Rugs, bedspreads,
pillows, and household
accessories.

La Victoriana
Hernandez Macias 72
152 6903
Botanical beauty
products, herbal
and homeopathic
remedies, flower
essence, and
aromatherapy.

La Zandunga
Hernandez Macias 129
152 4608
Fine Mexican rugs.

Mitu Atelier
Sollano 32
044 415 117 9431
Home accessories, custom furniture,
and antiques.

Productos Herco, S.A.
Relox 12
152 1434
A large selection of faucets, sinks,
bath tubs in various materials including copper and marble,
decorative hardware, and kitchen
accessories.

Sisal
Fabrica la Aurora
154 8944
Home decor and interior design.

Sollano 16
Sollano 16
154 8872
Lifestyle & home
décor and accessories.

Talavera Vázquez
Puebla No. 56
Delores Hidalgo, C.I.N., GTO.,
México
(418) 182 2914
Talavera tiles, flower pots, murals,
and earthenware.

Zocalo
Hernandez Macias 110
152 0663
Fine Mexican folk art and furniture, and hand-blown glassware.

Booksellers

Biblioteca Publica
Insurgentes 25
152 3770
Books, posters, guide books,
gift items, and cook books.

Casa de Papel
Mesones 57
154 5187
Greeting cards, journals, photo
albums, candles, guide books, road
maps, Mexican cook books, prints,
posters, and CDs.

El Colibri
Sollano 30
152 0751
Spanish language books, art books,
and artists' materials.

El Pato
M Ledesma 19
152 1543
Art supplies, design accessories.

Libreria la Deriva
Fabrica la Aurora
Art books, English and Spanish
language books.

Garrison & Garrison
Hernandez Macias 59
152 4547
New and second-hand books.

Lagundi
Umaran 17
152 0830
Art supplies, frames and framing,
posters, original prints, books,
and magazines.

Libros El Tecolote
Jesús 11
152 7395
English language books,
Mexican history, literature,
art & design books.

Wearable Art

Barbara Porter
Zacateros 47
152 7463
Fashion designs
for men & women.

Black & White
Loreto 20
154 4493
Traveling clothes, Alpaca sweaters,
and accessories.

Caracol Collection
Cuadrante 30
152 1617
Fine and applied art,
furniture, arte copper
and ceramics.

Christofas
Cuadrante 2
154 9392
Unique designer
jewelry, sculpture,
décor art, mobiles,
and gemstones.

Creación Marcela Andre
San Francisco 7
154 9868
Original art, jewelry,
and decorations.

Diva
Hernandez Macias 72
152 4980
Jewelry, accessories, and creative
quality clothes in European linens.

Girasol
Sn Francisco 72
152 2734
Mexican casuals.

Goldie Designs
Zacateros 19
154 7521
Classic clothing, elegant jewelry,
and custom accessories.

Nuevo México
Aparicio 1
152 4510
Navajo style crafts.

7th Heaven
Sollano 13
154 4677
Unique jewelry, art, gifts, & clothes.

Galleries

Akitsch
Pila Seca 16A
152 7343
Funky & kitsch jewelry,
accessories, & decoration.

Atenea Gallery
Jesús 2
152 0785
Paintings, sculpture, graphics,
jewelry, and art objects.

Azul Y Plata Disenos
Cuna de Allende 15
154 8192
Jewelry.

Casa Diana Art Gallery
Recreo 48
152 0885
Contemporary art.

Edgar Soberon
San Francisco 66
152 0306
Painting studio.

Estudio Ezcurdia
Fabrica la Aurora
152 6539
Paintings.

Galleria Anna Julia Agudo
Plaza Principal 18
Cell: 103 0228
Latin American art &
contemporary paintings.

Galería Aspen
Mesones 74
154 4441
Investment art.

Gallery Atotonilco
185 2225
Exceptional Mexican folk art, his-
toric photos, and vintage textiles.

Generator Gallery
Fabrica la Aurora
154 9588
Contemporary artists.

Galería Izamal
Mesones 80
154 5409
Paintings and jewelry design
by local artists.

Galería Mariposa
Recreo 36
152 4488
Specializing in one-of-a-kind
pieces by the great masters
of Mexican folk art.

Galería Pérgola
Instituto Allende
154 5595
Mexican fine art.

Mero
Zacateros 24
154 8580
Contemporary art.

Yam gallery
Institute Allende
Ancha de San Antonio
152 0338
Art & design.

ZOHO
Fabrica la Aurora
152 4791
A contemporary art gallery

Services

Fortuna
Pila Seca 3
152 7782
Conservation &
preservation of fine art,
photographs, textiles,
and memorabilia.

Information

Atencion
Insurgentes 25
152 3770
Weekly newspaper.

Promocion Mexican Culture
Hidalgo 18
152 0121

Tourist Information
Plaza Principal 10
120 4520

Bibliography

Barragan, The Complete Works. New York: Princeton Architectural Press, 1996.

de Haro, Fernando and Omar Fuentes. *Arquitectos Mexicanos, Una Visipn Contemporanea*. México D.F. Arquitectos Mexicanos Editores S.A. de C.V., 2004.

_____. *Mexican Interiors: Style & Personality*. México D.F.: Arquitectos Mexicanos Editores S.A. de C.V., 2003.

Levick, Melba and Gina Hyams. *Mexicasa, The Enchanting Inns and Haciendas of Mexico*. San Francisco: Chronicle Books, 2001.

_____. *In a Mexican Garden: Courtyards, Pools, and Open-Air Living Rooms*. San Francisco: Chronicle Books, 2005.

Levick, Melba, Tony Cohan and Masako Takahashi. *Mexicolor: The Spirit of Mexican Design*. San Francisco: Chronicle Books, 1998.

Luscombe-Whyte, Mark and Dominic Bradbury. *Mexico Architecture, Interiors & Design*. New York: Harper Collins Publishers, 2004.

Stoeltie, Barbara and Rene Stoeltie. *Living in Mexico: Vivre au Mexique:* Cologne: Taschen, 2004.

Streeter-Porter, Tim. *Casa Mexicana: The Architecture, Design and Style of Mexico*. New York: Stewart, Tabori & Chang, 1994.

Streeter-Porter, Tim, and Annie Kelly. *Casa Mexicana Style*. New York: Stewart, Tabori & Chang, 2006.

Villela, Khristaan, Ellen Bradbury and Logan Wagner. *Contemporary Mexican Design and Architecture*. Layton, Utah: Gibbs Smith, Publisher, 2002.

Yampolsky, Mariana and Chloe Sayer. *The Traditional Architecture of Mexico*. New York: Thames and Hudson, 1993.

Ypma, Herbert. *Mexican Contemporary*. New York: Stewart, Tabori & Chang, 1997.